The activities

- The activities in this book are desi_ to show whether your children ar 'ready' to read or are ready for a r difficult reading level. Their wish to read is the best sign of readiness.

- Many skills are involved, but most of them will be mastered unconsciously, just as your children learned to talk without direct teaching. They do not have to be equally good at, for instance, seeing letters distinctly, drawing, copying or telling a story. Success in particular activities should help you to find their strong points.

- The chart on page 32 details some of the skills and the ways these are linked with progress in learning to read.

The stories at Level 3

- These stories are still centred round the people who live in West Street, so your child has the fun and security of meeting the familiar characters again. These characters are also shown reading their own favourite books with their parents. The West Street 'children' like reading fairy stories, rhymes and legends. This emphasises how much all children enjoy reading and sharing stories with their parents, and how much this is a normal part of everyday life. It will also encourage your children to share their own enjoyment of the characters coming to life in these stories.

- Before you start reading the book with your child, read the story and activities first yourself, so that you become familiar with the text and the best

_ you can see the book easily. Read the story, making it sound as interesting as possible. Encourage your child to participate actively in the reading, to turn over the pages and to become involved in the story and characters. You may find that your child is ready to share in the reading more quickly than before.

- Sometimes let your children look through the book before you start reading, and for a change, let them guess what the story is about from the pictures. Encourage them to talk about the pictures, and add your own suggestions, if you wish, to help them with the story line.

- This may be enough for one sitting, but don't give your child the idea that the book is finished with. Encourage your child to take the book away and to look through it alone, to find any bits that either of you particularly enjoyed.

- Next time you look at the book with your child, suggest "Let's read the story together. You join in with me. If you want to go on reading on your own, give my arm a little push (or any other signal you prefer), and I'll stop reading and you go on. Give me another push when you want me to join in with you again." Let your child follow the words with a finger *under* them. Don't stop to repeat or correct words; keep the interest up and the story flowing along.

- The next time you both look at the book, have a quick chat about the contents of the story, then invite your child to read it to you without you reading as well. Give help with words or phrases that cause difficulty. Join in with the reading again if your child is struggling with the story.

The activities at Level 3

- The activities at the back of the book need not be completed at once. They are not a test, but will help your child to remember the words and stories and to develop further skills required for becoming a fluent reader.

  The activities are often divided into three parts.

- One part is designed to encourage you both to talk about the stories, and to link them where possible with your child's own experiences. Encourage your child to predict what will happen and to recall the main events of the story. Change the wording of the story as much as you like and encourage your children to tell you about the story in their own way.

- One part encourages children to look back through the book to find general or specific things in the text or the pictures. Your child learns to begin to look at the text itself, and to recognise individual words and letters more precisely. The activities state clearly when you should give a letter its name, and when you should sound it out. The activities also introduce more writing, largely copying from words in the original story. If your children find this too difficult, copy the words onto a piece of paper for them to trace over.

- One part includes activities which your child can do without your help. It may be necessary, though, to read the instructions to the child, pointing out the words as you do so. Read the instructions to the *first* activity only in this way. Then say "Would you like to try this on your own?" One activity at a time is probably enough for your child to do in one sitting.

- When all the activities have been done, encourage your child to read the story again before you move on to another book. Your child should now feel secure with it and enjoy reading to you.

BEFORE READING THE STORY. Turn to page 28 and do the first activity with your child.

The obstacle race

Illustrated by Tony Kenyon

A Piccolo Original
In association with Macmillan Education

Come to our obstacle race.

What is an obstacle race?
Come and see.

Come to our obstacle race.

What is an obstacle race?
Come and see.

It was the day of the race.

Mr Maggs told the children what to do.

First, jump over the rope.

Then crawl under the net.

Get into the sack.

Put on a hat and
a pair of gloves.

Run to the tape.

Line up, children.

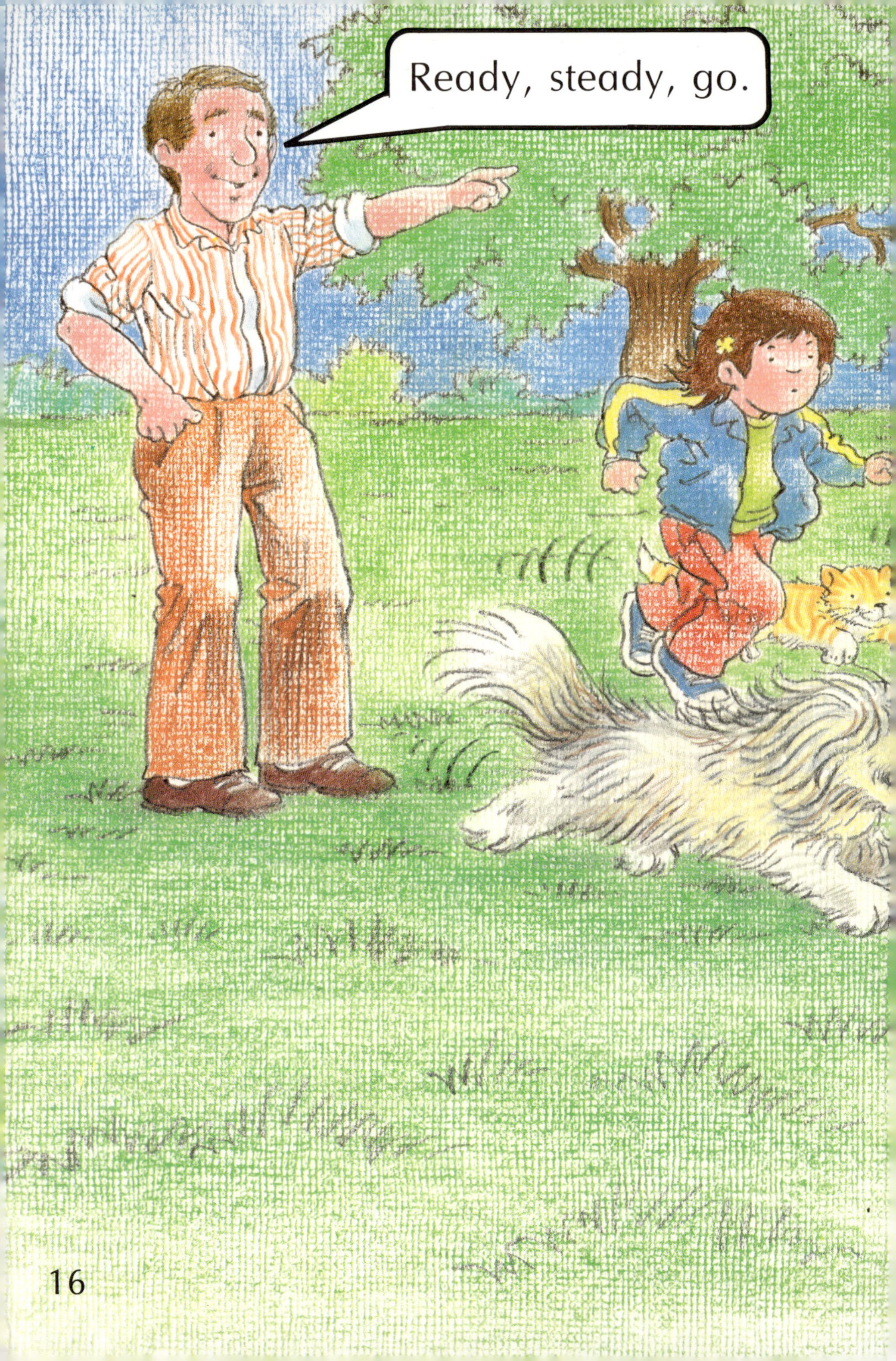
Ready, steady, go.

Ready, steady, go.

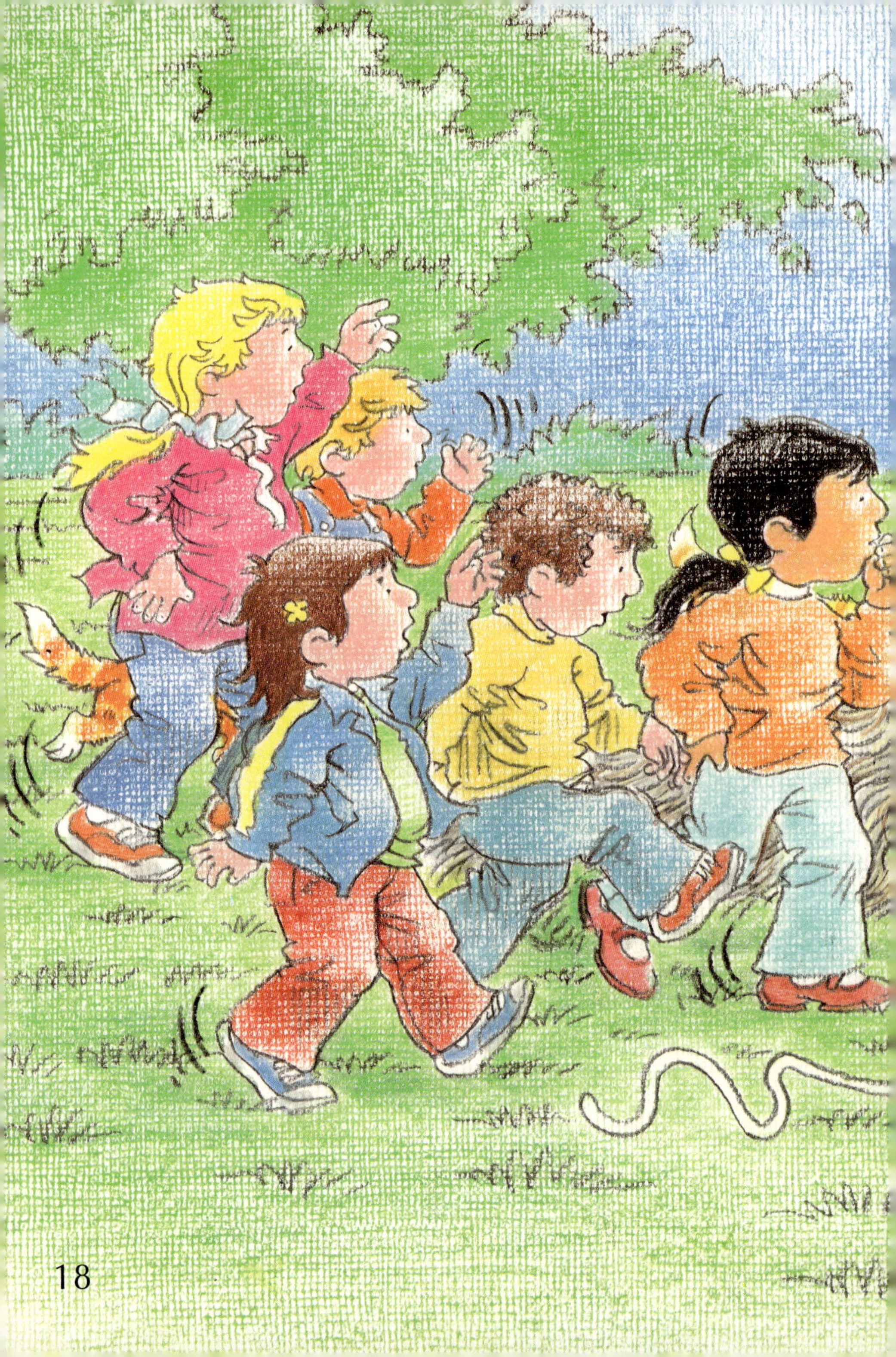

Oh dear.
Dennis has taken the rope.

Mind my hair.
Get off my foot.

Go away, Ginger.
I can't get out.

It's dirty.
I've lost my shoe.

I can't get in.
Go away, Moo.

That's my glove.
I want that hat.

I can't see a thing.
Hurry up, children.

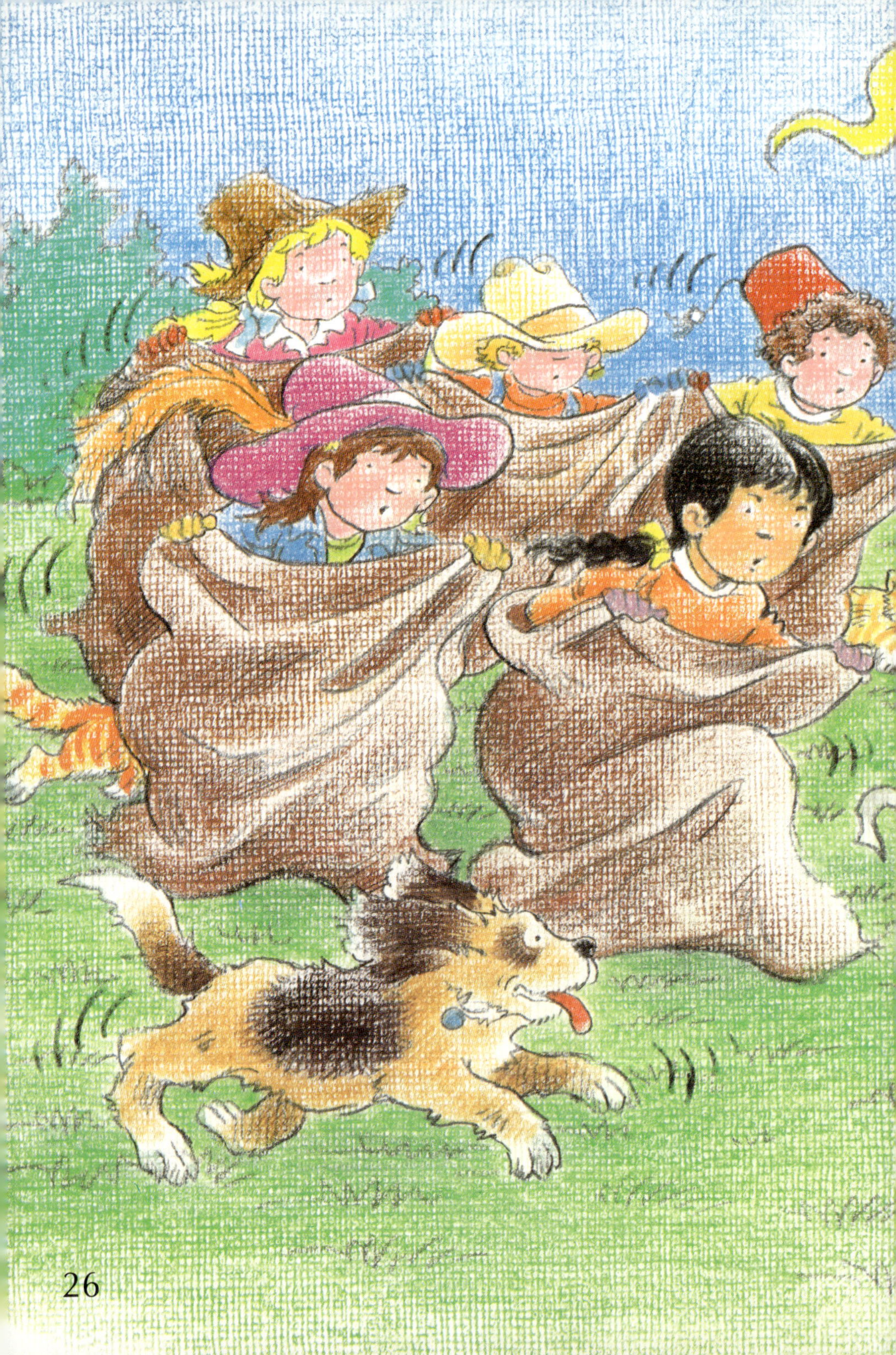

Tops has won the obstacle race.

Things to talk about with your children

1. Let's look at the cover of the book before we read it.
   What do you think the story is going to be about?
   Who do you think will be in the story?

2. Do you know what each of these races is called? Do you know what you have to do for each one?

3. Can you think of some other things that Mr Maggs could have put in the obstacle race?

Looking at pictures and words with your children

1. Here are some of the things that Mr Maggs told the children to do in the obstacle race, but they are all in the wrong order. Can you read them out in the order they came in the story?

Run to the tape.

Crawl under the net.

Put on a hat and
a pair of gloves.

Jump over the rope.

2. How many times can you find the word obstacle in the story?
   Do you know what its first letter is called?

   Can you find any other words that begin with O
   Can you read them to me?

3. Look at these bits from the story.

   Come and see.

   Go away, Tops.

   Ready, steady, go.

   How quickly can you find the page numbers for these bits from the story?

4. Can you find the missing letter in these words?

   r__ce   h__t   s__ck   t__pe

   Now try to find this missing letter.

   j__mp   __nder   h__rry   r__n

5. I'll read these sentences to you. Can you tell me which of them are true? Which are not true?

   The race was in Tamla's garden.
   Mr Maggs told the children what to do.
   The animals joined in the race.
   Dennis won the obstacle race.
   Len's hat was too small.

Things for your child to do

Draw a picture of Tops and write Tops on the back of it.

Now draw a picture of Dennis on another piece of paper and write Dennis on the back of it.

Cut out the pictures of the dogs and put them in a starting line on the floor.
Decide where the finishing line is and we'll have a race.
You choose one dog and I'll choose the other. We'll make the dogs move along the floor by flapping a folded newspaper behind each picture. Which dog will win?

These activities and skills:	will help your children to:
Looking and remembering	hold a story in their heads, retell it in their own words.
Listening, being able to tell the difference between sounds	remember sounds in words and link spoken words with the words they see in print.
Naming things and using different words to explain or retell events	recognise different words in print, build their vocabulary and guess at the meaning of words.
Matching, seeing patterns, similarities and differences	recognise letters, see patterns within words, use the patterns to read 'new' words and split long words into syllables.
Knowing the grammatical patterns of spoken language	guess the word-order in reading.
Anticipating what is likely to happen next in a story	guess what the next sentence or event is likely to be about.
Colouring, getting control of pencils and pens, copying and spelling	produce their own writing, which will help them to understand the way English is written.
Understanding new experiences by linking them to what they already know	read with understanding and think about what they have read.
Understanding their own feelings and those of others	enjoy and respond to stories and identify with the characters.

First published 1990 by Pan Books Ltd,
Cavaye Place, London SW10 9PG

9 8 7 6 5 4 3 2 1

Editorial consultant: Donna Bailey

© Pan Books Ltd and Macmillan Publishers Ltd 1990. Text © Helen Arnold 1990

British Library Cataloguing in Publication Data
Arnold, Helen
The obstacle race.
1. English language. Readers — For children
I. Title II. Series
428.6
ISBN 0-330-30699-5

Printed in Hong Kong

This book is sold subject to the condition that it shall not, by way of trade or otherwise be lent, re-sold, hired out or otherwise circulated without the publisher's prior consent in any form of binding or cover other than that in which it is published and without a similar condition including this condition being imposed on the subsequent purchaser

Whilst the advice and information in this book are believed to be true and accurate at the time of going to press, neither the author nor the publisher can accept any legal responsibility or liability for any errors or omissions that may be made

IT'S ALL ABOUT JESUS!

realfaith.com